National 5 Physics
250 Practice Questions on Electric Circuits
(2023)

Published in Great Britain in 2023

ISBN **9798397781558**

Text and Illustrations Copyright © James Harding

Other books by James Harding

National 5 Physics – 200 Practice Questions on Mechanics (2023)
National 5 Physics – 200 Practice Questions on Radioactivity (2022)
National 5 Chemistry – 225 Practice Questions on Atomic Structure and Radioactivity (2022)

DID YOU LIKE THIS BOOK?

If you liked this book, consider giving it a review where you bought it. This will help others to find the book.

National 5 Physics
250 Practice Questions on Electric Circuits
(2023)

1.) What type of circuit component does the symbol below represent?

   i.) a resistor   iii.) a wire

   ii.) a cell   iv.) a fuse

[1 mark]

2.) What type of circuit component does the symbol below represent?

   i.) a filament lamp / bulb   iii.) a wire

   ii.) a cell   iv.) a fuse

[1 mark]

3.) What type of circuit component does the symbol below represent?

   i.) a wire   iii.) a battery

   ii.) a filament lamp / bulb   iv.) a fuse

[1 mark]

4.) What type of circuit component does the symbol below represent?

   i.) a fuse   iii.) a filament lamp / bulb

   ii.) a cell   iv.) a resistor

[1 mark]

5.) What type of circuit component does the symbol below represent?

i.) a battery   iii.) a wire

ii.) a filament lamp / bulb   iv.) a fuse

[1 mark]

6.) Does the symbol below represent an **open switch** or a **closed switch**?

i.) a closed switch   ii.) an open switch

[1 mark]

7.) The diagram below shows an incomplete circuit. Complete the circuit by drawing a **resistor** between the open ends of the wires.

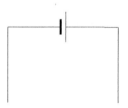

[1 mark]

8.) The diagram below shows an incomplete circuit. Complete the circuit by drawing a **filament lamp** between the open ends of the wires.

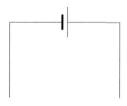

[1 mark]

9.) The diagram below shows an incomplete circuit. Complete the circuit by drawing a **battery** between the open ends of the wires.

[1 mark]

10.) The diagram below shows a circuit. Is the circuit **complete**?

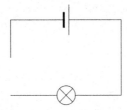

    i.) Yes   ii.) No

[1 mark]

11.) The diagram below shows a circuit. Is the circuit **complete**?

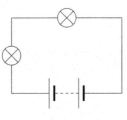

    i.) Yes   ii.) No

[1 mark]

12.) The diagram below shows a circuit. Is the circuit **complete**?

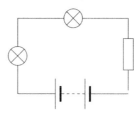

   i.) Yes   ii.) No

[1 mark]

13.) The diagram below shows a circuit. Will there be a current in the circuit?

   i.) Yes   ii.) No

[1 mark]

14.) The diagram below shows a circuit. Will there be a current in the circuit?

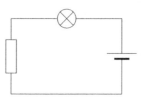

   i.) Yes   ii.) No

[1 mark]

15.) The diagram below shows a circuit. Will there be a current in the circuit?

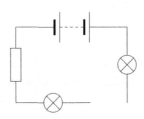

   i.) Yes   ii.) No

                                                  [1 mark]

16.) The diagram below shows a circuit. Will there be a current in the circuit?

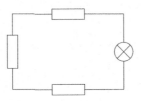

   i.) Yes   ii.) No

                                                  [1 mark]

17.) The diagram below shows a circuit. Will there be a current in the circuit?

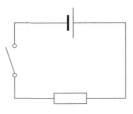

   i.) Yes   ii.) No

                                                  [1 mark]

18.) Below are shown two circuit diagrams. Are the circuit diagrams **equivalent**?

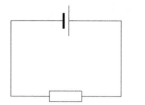 

i.) Yes   ii.) No

[1 mark]

19.) Below are shown two circuit diagrams. Are the circuit diagrams **equivalent**?

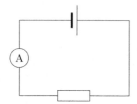 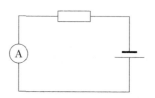

i.) Yes   ii.) No

[1 mark]

20.) Below are shown two circuit diagrams. Are the circuit diagrams **equivalent**?

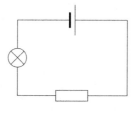 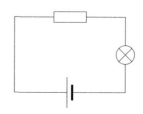

i.) Yes   ii.) No

[1 mark]

21.) Below are shown two circuit diagrams. Are the circuit diagrams **equivalent**?

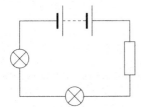 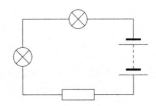

i.) Yes   ii.) No

[1 mark]

22.) What type of circuit component does the symbol below represent?

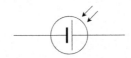

i.) a battery   iii.) a filament lamp / bulb

ii.) a photovoltaic cell   iv.) a fuse

[1 mark]

23.) What type of circuit component does the symbol below represent?

i.) a wire   iii.) a diode

ii.) a battery   iv.) a cell

[1 mark]

24.) What type of circuit component does the symbol below represent?

  i.) a light-emitting diode   iii.) a resistor

  ii.) a wire   iv.) a battery

[1 mark]

25.) What type of circuit component does the symbol below represent?

  i.) a fuse

  ii.) a light-emitting diode

  iii.) a thermistor

  iv.) a variable resistor

[1 mark]

26.) What type of circuit component does the symbol below represent?

  i.) a thermistor

  ii.) a fuse

  iii.) a variable resistor

  iv.) a diode

[1 mark]

27.) What type of circuit component does the symbol below represent?

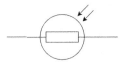

   i.) a diode

  ii.) a light-emitting diode

 iii.) a light-dependent resistor

 iv.) a variable resistor

[1 mark]

28.) The diagram below shows an incomplete circuit. Complete the circuit by drawing a **light-emitting diode** between the open ends of the wires.

[1 mark]

29.) The diagram below shows an incomplete circuit. Complete the circuit by drawing a **variable resistor** between the open ends of the wires.

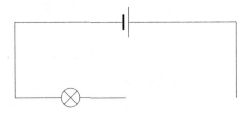

[1 mark]

30.) What type of circuit component does the symbol below represent?

    i.) a capacitor   iii.) a photovoltaic cell

    ii.) a battery   iv.) a filament lamp / bulb

[1 mark]

31.) The diagram below shows a circuit. Are the two resistors in the circuit connected **in series** or **in parallel** with each other?

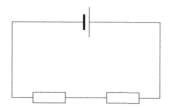

    i.) in parallel   ii.) in series

[1 mark]

32.) The diagram below shows a circuit. Are the two resistors in the circuit connected **in series** or **in parallel** with each other?

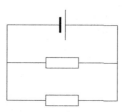

    i.) in parallel   ii.) in series

[1 mark]

33.) The diagram below shows a circuit. Are the two resistors in the circuit connected **in series** or **in parallel** with each other?

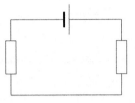

   i.) in series   ii.) in parallel

[1 mark]

34.) The diagram below shows a circuit. Are the two resistors in the circuit connected **in series** or **in parallel** with each other?

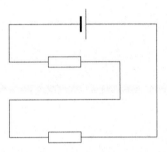

   i.) in parallel   ii.) in series

[1 mark]

35.) The diagram below shows an incomplete circuit. Complete the circuit by drawing a filament lamp and a resistor **in series** with each other and with the cell.

[1 mark]

36.) The diagram below shows an incomplete circuit. Complete the circuit by drawing two filament lamps **in parallel** with each other and with the cell.

[1 mark]

37.) The diagram below shows an incomplete circuit. Complete the circuit by drawing a resistor and a closed switch **in series** with each other and with the cell.

[1 mark]

38.) Complete the following sentence.

Electric current is the flow of _____.

[1 mark]

39.) Which of the following statements is correct?

i.) In a circuit that has an electric current, the negatively-charged electrons in the wire **do** move, but the positively-charged atomic nuclei **don't** move.

ii.) In a circuit that has an electric current, the negatively-charged electrons in the wire **don't** move, but the positively-charged atomic nuclei **do** move.

iii.) In a circuit that has an electric current, **both** the negatively-charged electrons and the positively-charged atomic nuclei in the wire move.

[1 mark]

40.) What is the S.I. unit of **electric charge**?

_____

[1 mark]

41.) What is the S.I. unit of **electric current**?

_____

[1 mark]

42.) Complete the following sentence.

One _____ of charge moving past a point in a circuit in one _____ is one _____ of current.

[1 mark]

43.) Write the symbol for **coulombs**?

_____

[1 mark]

44.) Write the symbol for **amperes**?

_____

[1 mark]

45.) Which of the following is the correct symbol for **seconds**?

i.) t   ii.) T   iii.) S   iv.) s

[1 mark]

46.) How many millicoulombs are there in 1 coulomb?

i.) 1000   ii.) 10000   iii.) 10   iv.) 1000000

[1 mark]

47.) How many milliamperes are there in 1 ampere?

i.) 100   ii.) 10000   iii.) 1000000   iv.) 1000

[1 mark]

48.) Which of the following is the correct symbol for **millicoulombs**?

i.) mC   iii.) C   v.) mc

ii.) c   iv.) MC   vi.) Mc

[1 mark]

49.) Which of the following is the correct symbol for **milliamperes**?

i.) mA   iii.) ma   v.) Ma

ii.) MA   iv.) a   vi.) A

[1 mark]

50.) Which of the following are measures of **electric charge**?

i.) $130\,\Omega$ iv.) $24.5\,\text{M}\Omega$ vii.) $30\,\text{V}$ x.) $0.65\,\text{A}$

ii.) $650\,\Omega$ v.) $21.9\,\text{k}\Omega$ viii.) $1150\,\text{mC}$ xi.) $2.3\,\text{V}$

iii.) $22.4\,\text{C}$ vi.) $285\,\text{C}$ ix.) $248\,\text{mC}$ xii.) $88\,\text{kV}$

[1 mark]

51.) Which of the following are measures of **electric current**?

i.) $261\,\text{mA}$ iv.) $291\,\text{C}$ vii.) $14.2\,\text{kV}$ x.) $0.71\,\text{A}$

ii.) $21.8\,\text{C}$ v.) $28\,\text{V}$ viii.) $2.1\,\text{V}$ xi.) $19.5\,\text{M}\Omega$

iii.) $1.1\,\text{A}$ vi.) $24\,\text{k}\Omega$ ix.) $1850\,\Omega$ xii.) $226\,\text{mA}$

[1 mark]

52.) What is $6785\,\text{mC}$ in coulombs?

i.) $6.785\,\text{C}$ ii.) $0.06785\,\text{C}$ iii.) $0.6785\,\text{C}$ iv.) $678.5\,\text{C}$

[1 mark]

53.) What is $9305\,\text{mC}$ in coulombs?

_____

[1 mark]

54.) What is $119.3\,\text{C}$ in millicoulombs?

  i.) $119.3\,\text{mC}$ ii.) $1193000\,\text{mC}$ iii.) $1193\,\text{mC}$ iv.) $119300\,\text{mC}$

[1 mark]

55.) What is $23.6\,\text{C}$ in millicoulombs?

_____

[1 mark]

56.) What is $8680\,\text{mA}$ in amperes?

  i.) $8.68\,\text{A}$ ii.) $0.868\,\text{A}$ iii.) $86.8\,\text{A}$ iv.) $0.00868\,\text{A}$

[1 mark]

57.) What is $5085\,\text{mA}$ in amperes?

_____

[1 mark]

58.) What is $7.96\,\text{A}$ in milliamperes?

  i.) $796000\,\text{mA}$ ii.) $79600\,\text{mA}$ iii.) $796\,\text{mA}$ iv.) $7960\,\text{mA}$

[1 mark]

59.) What is $3.01\,\text{A}$ in milliamperes?

_____

[1 mark]

60.) What is **direct current**?

_____

_____

[2 marks]

61.) What is **alternating current**?

_____

_____

[3 marks]

62.) The graph below shows the current at a point in a circuit over time.

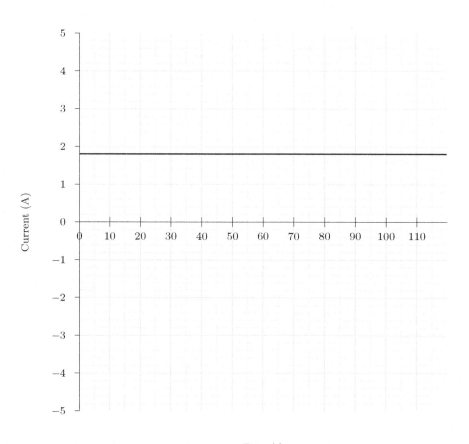

Time (s)

What **type** of current does the graph show?

i.) alternating current   ii.) direct current

[1 mark]

63.) The graph below shows the current at a point in a circuit over time.

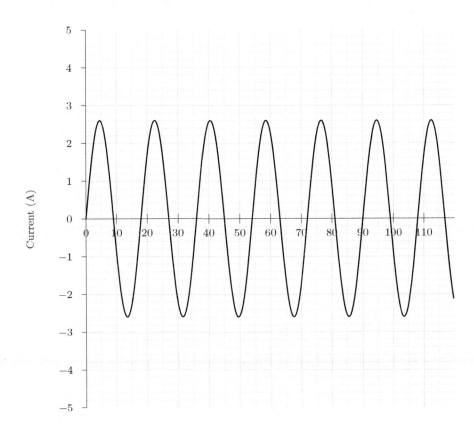

Time (s)

What **type** of current does the graph show?

   i.) direct current   ii.) alternating current

[1 mark]

64.) The graph below shows the current at a point in a circuit over time.

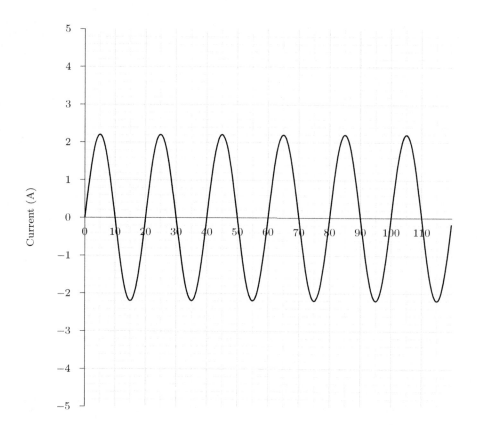

What **type** of current does the graph show?

   i.) alternating current   ii.) direct current

[1 mark]

65.) The graph below shows the current at a point in a circuit over time.

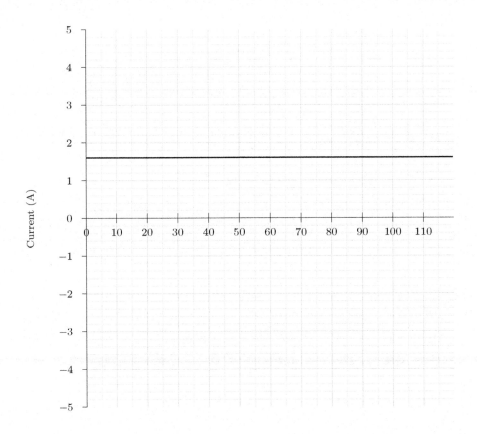

Time (s)

What **type** of current does the graph show?

i.) direct current   ii.) alternating current

[1 mark]

66.) What type of current does a **cell** provide?

i.) direct current   ii.) alternating current

[1 mark]

67.) What type of current does a **mains electricity** provide?

i.) alternating current   ii.) direct current

[1 mark]

68.) The symbol below represents a cell. Label the positive and negative terminals of the cell with plus and minus signs.

[1 mark]

69.) The diagram below shows a circuit consisting of a cell and a resistor connected in series.

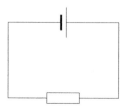

a.) What is the direction of the **conventional current** in the circuit?

   i.) clockwise   ii.) anticlockwise

[1 mark]

b.) What is the direction of the **electron flow** in the circuit?

   i.) clockwise   ii.) anticlockwise

[1 mark]

70.) The diagram below shows a circuit consisting of a cell and a resistor connected in series.

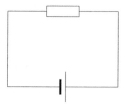

a.) What is the direction of the **conventional current** in the circuit?

   i.) anticlockwise   ii.) clockwise

[1 mark]

b.) What is the direction of the **electron flow** in the circuit?

i.) anticlockwise

ii.) clockwise

[1 mark]

71.) The diagram below shows a circuit consisting of a cell and two resistors connected in series.

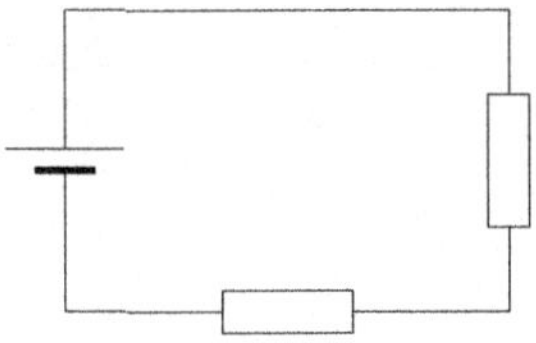

a.) What is the direction of the **conventional current** in the circuit?

i.) anticlockwise

ii.) clockwise

[1 mark]

b.) What is the direction of the **electron flow** in the circuit?

i.) clockwise

ii.) anticlockwise

[1 mark]

72.) Which of the following statements is correct?

i.) The conventional current in a circuit is in the **opposite direction** to the motion of the electrons.

ii.) The conventional current in a circuit is in the **same direction** to the motion of the electrons.

[1 mark]

73.) What type of circuit component does the symbol below represent?

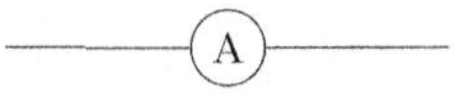

i.) a galvanometer

iii.) a battery

ii.) an ammeter

iv.) a resistor

[1 mark]

74.) Which of the following statements is true?

i.) In order to measure the current through a component, an ammeter must be connected **in parallel** with the component.

ii.) In order to measure the current through a component, an ammeter must be connected **in series** with the component.

[**1 mark**]

75.) The diagram below shows a cell and a bulb.

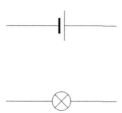

Draw wires on the diagram to connect the bulb across the cell, adding an ammeter that would measure the current through the bulb.

[**2 marks**]

76.) The diagram below shows a circuit consisting of a battery and a bulb connected in series. If 345 C of charge passes through the bulb in 75 s, what is the current in the bulb?

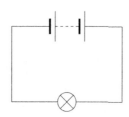

_____

[**2 marks**]

77.) 800 C of charge passes through a bulb in a circuit in 100 s. What is the current in the bulb?

_____

[**2 marks**]

78.) The diagram below shows a circuit . If the current in the resistor is 0.5 A for 170 s, how much charge passes through the resistor?

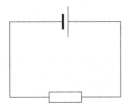

[2 marks]

79.) 5.5 C of charge passes through a bulb in a circuit in 5 s. What is the current in the bulb?

[2 marks]

80.) The diagram below shows a circuit consisting of a cell and a resistor connected in series. If the current in the bulb is 7.2 A, how long does it take for 108 C of charge to pass through the resistor?

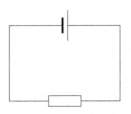

[2 marks]

81.) The current in a resistor in a circuit is 4.4 A. How long does it take for 352 C of charge to pass through the resistor?

[2 marks]

82.) The current in a bulb in a circuit is 0.4 A. How much charge passes through the bulb in 175 s?

_____

[2 marks]

83.) 1320 C of charge passes through a bulb in a circuit in 5 min. What is the current in the bulb?

_____

[3 marks]

84.) The current in a bulb in a circuit is 2.9 A. How long does it take for 9657 C of charge to pass through the bulb?

_____

[3 marks]

85.) The current in a resistor in a circuit is 4.2 A. How much charge passes through the resistor in 18.5 min?

_____

[3 marks]

86.) 23800 mC of charge passes through a resistor in a circuit in 119 s. Calculate the current in the resistor. Give your answer in milliamperes.

_____

[3 marks]

87.) What is a **diode**?

_____

_____

[2 marks]

88.) What is a **light-emitting diode**?

_____

_____

[2 marks]

89.) The diagram below shows a circuit. Will there be a current in the circuit?

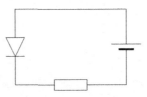

   i.) Yes   ii.) No

[1 mark]

90.) The diagram below shows a circuit. Will there be a current in the circuit?

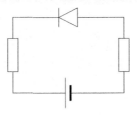

   i.) Yes   ii.) No

[1 mark]

91.) The diagram below shows a circuit. Will there be a current in the circuit?

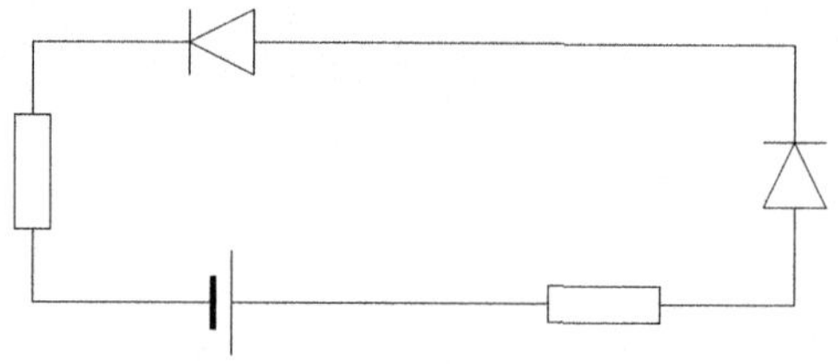

i.) Yes   ii.) No

[1 mark]

92.) The diagram below shows a circuit. Will there be a current in the circuit?

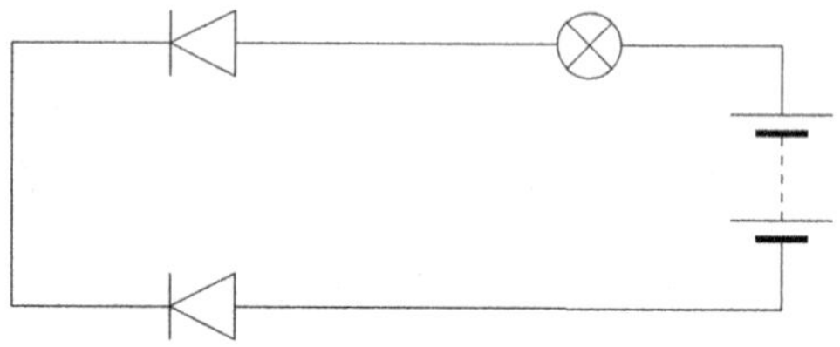

i.) Yes   ii.) No

[1 mark]

93.) Describe what **electrical resistance** is.

_____

_____

_____

[2 marks]

94.) What is the S.I. unit of **electrical resistance**?

_____

[1 mark]

95.) Below is shown a Greek letter.

$$\Omega$$

What is the name of this letter?

    i.) omega   iii.) ohm   v.) oo

    ii.) omicron   iv.) psi   vi.) phi

[1 mark]

96.) Which of the following is the correct symbol for **ohms**?

    i.) ρ iii.) ω v.) o

    ii.) Ω iv.) O   vi.) r

[1 mark]

97.) How many ohms are there in 1 kilo-ohm?

    i.) 100   ii.) 1000   iii.) 10   iv.) 1000000

[1 mark]

98.) How many kilo-ohms are there in 1 mega-ohm?

    i.) 100000   ii.) 10   iii.) 1000   iv.) 100

[1 mark]

99.) How many ohms are there in 1 mega-ohm?

    i.) 1000000   ii.) 10000000   iii.) 1000   iv.) 10

[1 mark]

100.) Which of the following is the correct symbol for **kilo-ohms**?

    i.) KO   iii.) kΩ v.) kO

    ii.) Ko   iv.) KΩ vi.) ko

[1 mark]

101.) Which of the following is the correct symbol for **mega-ohms**?

i.) mo   iii.) Mo   v.) MO

ii.) mΩ iv.) mO   vi.) MΩ

[1 mark]

102.) Which of the following are measures of **electrical resistance**?

i.) 60 C   iv.) 25.1 kΩ vii.) 9.9 MΩ x.) 29 V

ii.) 1.6 C   v.) 475 Ω viii.) 2.7 A   xi.) 920 Ω

iii.) 2.5 kV   vi.) 262 mC   ix.) 129 kV   xii.) 230 mA

[1 mark]

103.) What is 32.6 kΩ in ohms?

i.) 326000 Ω ii.) 32600 Ω iii.) 32.6 Ω iv.) 3260000 Ω

[1 mark]

104.) What is 18.9 kΩ in ohms?

_____

[1 mark]

105.) What is 20000 Ω in kilo-ohms?

i.) 2 kΩ ii.) 20 kΩ iii.) 2000 kΩ iv.) 200 kΩ

[1 mark]

106.) What is 78000 Ω in kilo-ohms?

_____

[1 mark]

107.) What is 77000 kΩ in mega-ohms?

i.) 77 MΩ ii.) 7.7 MΩ iii.) 0.077 MΩ iv.) 7700 MΩ

[1 mark]

108.) What is $43000\,k\Omega$ in mega-ohms?

_____

[1 mark]

109.) What is $63.7\,M\Omega$ in ohms?

   i.) $6.37 \times 10^7\,\Omega$ ii.) $63700\,\Omega$ iii.) $6.37 \times 10^9\,\Omega$ iv.) $6370000\,\Omega$

[1 mark]

110.) What is $62.5\,M\Omega$ in ohms?

_____

[1 mark]

111.) What is $2.9 \times 10^7\,\Omega$ in mega-ohms?

   i.) $0.029\,M\Omega$ ii.) $29\,M\Omega$ iii.) $290\,M\Omega$ iv.) $29000\,M\Omega$

[1 mark]

112.) What is $7000000\,\Omega$ in mega-ohms?

_____

[1 mark]

113.) Which of the following is a type of device used for measuring electrical resistance?

   i.) a galvanometer   iii.) an ohmmeter

   ii.) an ammeter   iv.) a voltmeter

[1 mark]

114.) What type of circuit component does the symbol below represent?

———$\left(\Omega\right)$———

   i.) an ohmmeter   iii.) an ammeter

   ii.) a resistor   iv.) a voltmeter

[1 mark]

115.) What is the S.I. unit of **electric potential difference**?

_____

[**1 mark**]

116.) Write the symbol for **volts**?

_____

[**1 mark**]

117.) What is 22.1 kV in volts?

  i.) 2.21×10^7 V   ii.) 221 V   iii.) 221000 V   iv.) 22100 V

[**1 mark**]

118.) What is 7.4 kV in volts?

_____

[**1 mark**]

119.) What is 6000 V in kilovolts?

  i.) 6000 kV   ii.) 60 kV   iii.) 0.06 kV   iv.) 6 kV

[**1 mark**]

120.) What is 10200 V in kilovolts?

_____

[**1 mark**]

121.) What type of circuit component does the symbol below represent?

—————(V)—————

  i.) a voltmeter   iii.) a wire

  ii.) a battery   iv.) a fuse

[**1 mark**]

122.) Which of the following statements is true?

   i.) In order to measure the potential difference across a component, a voltmeter must be connected **in series** with the component.

   ii.) In order to measure the potential difference across a component, a voltmeter must be connected **in parallel** with the component.

[1 mark]

123.) The circuit diagram below shows a bulb connected in series with a cell.

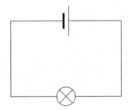

Add a voltmeter to the circuit diagram that would measure the potential difference across the bulb.

[2 marks]

124.) a.) Which of the following formulae correctly relates the current through a component, I, to the potential difference across the component, V, and the resistance of the component, R?

   i.) $I = \frac{V}{R}$ iii.) $I = V + R$

   ii.) $I = VR$ iv.) $I = VR^2$

[1 mark]

b.) What is the name of this relation?

   i.) Kirchhoff's Law   iii.) Joule's Law

   ii.) Coulomb's Law   iv.) Ohm's Law

[1 mark]

125.) The diagram below shows a circuit.

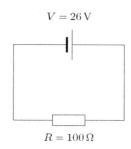

Work out the current in the resistor.

i.) 0.26 A   ii.) 126 A   iii.) 0.76 A   iv.) 1.26 A

[2 marks]

126.) The formula $I = \frac{V}{R}$ relates the current through a component, I, to the potential difference across it, V, and its resistance, R. Which of the following is the same formula, rearranged to make R the subject?

i.) $R = V^2 I$ iii.) $R = \frac{I}{V}$

ii.) $R = \frac{V}{I}$ iv.) $R = V + I$

[1 mark]

127.) The diagram below shows a circuit.

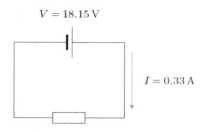

Determine the resistance of the resistor.

i.) 5.9895 Ω   ii.) 105 Ω   iii.) 55 Ω   iv.) 18.48 Ω

[2 marks]

128.) The formula $I = \frac{V}{R}$ relates the current through a component, I, to the potential difference across it, V, and its resistance, R. Which of the following is the same formula, rearranged to make V the subject?

i.) $V = I + R$ iii.) $V = IR$

ii.) $V = IR^2$ iv.) $V = \frac{I}{R}$

[1 mark]

129.) The diagram below shows a circuit.

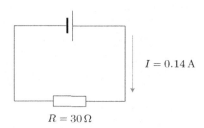

$I = 0.14\,\text{A}$

$R = 30\,\Omega$

Calculate the potential difference provided by the cell.

i.) $7.2\,\text{V}$ ii.) $4.2\,\text{V}$ iii.) $0.588\,\text{V}$ iv.) $30.14\,\text{V}$

[2 marks]

130.) A circuit consists of a bulb connected across a cell. The resistance of the bulb is $65\,\Omega$, and the current through it is $0.38\,\text{A}$. Determine the potential difference provided by the cell.

_____

[3 marks]

131.) A circuit consists of a bulb connected across a battery. The potential difference provided by the battery is $10.8\,\text{V}$, and the bulb has a resistance of $30\,\Omega$. What is the current through the bulb?

_____

[3 marks]

132.) A circuit consists of a resistor connected across a battery. The potential difference provided by the battery is 44.65 V, and the current through the resistor is 0.47 A. What is the resistance of the resistor?

_____

[3 marks]

133.) Imogen sets up the circuit shown in the diagram below. The reading on the ammeter is 0.23 A, and the reading on the voltmeter is 39.1 V. What is the resistance of the resistor?

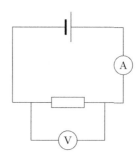

i.) 8.993 Ω   ii.) 170 Ω   iii.) 38.87 Ω   iv.) 39.33 Ω

[2 marks]

134.) a.) In the space below, draw a diagram for a circuit that consists of a filament lamp connected across a battery.

[2 marks]

b.) If the filament lamp has a resistance of 345 Ω, and the battery provides a potential difference of 100.05 V, what is the current through the lamp?

_____

[3 marks]

c.) How much charge passes through the filament lamp in 290 s?

_____

[3 marks]

135.) A student sets up a circuit consisting of a resistor connected across a cell. He uses an ammeter to measure the current in the circuit, and a voltmeter to measure the potential difference across the resistor. Then he changes the cell for a different one, and measures the current and potential difference again. He does this several times. His results are shown in the table below.

Potential Difference (V)	Current (A)
20	0.4
40	0.8
60	1.2
80	1.6
100	2

What is the resistance of the resistor?

_____

[4 marks]

136.) A student sets up a circuit consisting of a resistor connected across a cell. She uses an ammeter to measure the current in the circuit, and a voltmeter to measure the potential difference across the resistor. Then she changes the cell for a different one, and measures the current and potential difference again. She does this several times, writing down her results. She then plots the results on a graph, which is shown below.

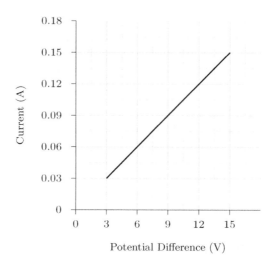

What is the resistance of the resistor?

_____

[4 marks]

137.) Which of the following formulae correctly relates the total resistance, R_{total}, of resistors connected in series to the resistances, R_1, R_2, R_3, et cetera, of each resistor?

i.) $\frac{1}{R_{total}} = \frac{1}{R_1} + \frac{1}{R_2} + \frac{1}{R_3} + ...$

ii.) $R_{total} = R_1 + R_2 + R_3 + ...$

iii.) $R_{total} = \frac{1}{R_1} + \frac{1}{R_2} + \frac{1}{R_3} + ...$

iv.) $R_{total} = \frac{R_1 + R_2 + R_3 + ...}{R_1 \times R_2 \times R_3 \times ...}$

[1 mark]

138.) The diagram below shows a circuit. What is the total resistance of the two resistors in the circuit?

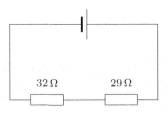

[2 marks]

139.) The diagram below shows a circuit. What is the total resistance of the two resistors in the circuit?

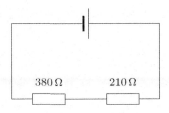

[2 marks]

140.) The diagram below shows a circuit. What is the total resistance of the two resistors in the circuit?

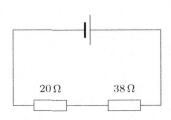

[2 marks]

141.) The diagram below shows a circuit. What is the total resistance of the three resistors in the circuit?

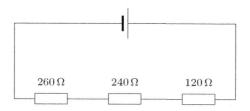

[2 marks]

142.) The diagram below shows a circuit. The total resistance of the two resistors is $54\,\Omega$. What is the value of R?

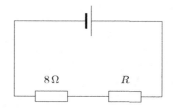

[2 marks]

143.) The diagram below shows a circuit. The total resistance of the three resistors is $980\,\Omega$. What is the value of R?

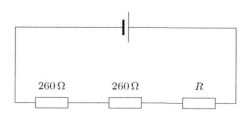

[2 marks]

144.) The diagram below shows a circuit. The two resistors in the circuit are identical, each having a resistance R. The total resistance of the two resistors is $70\,\Omega$. What is the value of R?

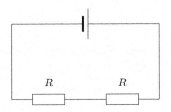

[2 marks]

145.) The diagram below shows a circuit. The four resistors in the circuit are identical, each having a resistance R. The total resistance of the four resistors is $1280\,\Omega$. What is the value of R?

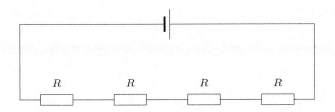

[2 marks]

146.) The diagram below shows a circuit. The reading on the first ammeter, I_1, is 0.01 A. What is the reading on the second ammeter, I_2?

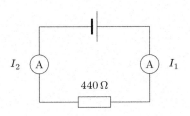

[2 marks]

147.) The diagram below shows a circuit. The reading on the first ammeter, I_1, is 0.88 A. What is the reading on the second ammeter, I_2?

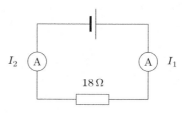

[2 marks]

148.) The diagram below shows a circuit. The reading on the first ammeter, I_1, is 0.88 A.

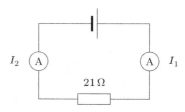

Which of the following algebraic expressions is correct?

i.) $I_1 > I_2$ iii.) $I_1 < I_2$

ii.) $I_1 = I_2$

[3 marks]

149.) The diagram below shows a circuit. The reading on the first ammeter, I_1, is 0.27 A.

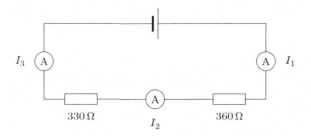

Which of the following algebraic expressions is correct?

i.) $I_1 > I_2 > I_3$

iii.) $I_2 > I_3 > I_1$

ii.) $I_1 = I_2 = I_3$

iv.) $I_2 > I_1 > I_3$

[3 marks]

150.) The diagram below shows a circuit. The potential difference provided by the cell, V_{cell}, is 30 V, and the potential difference across the first resistor, V_1, is 24 V. What is the potential difference across the second resistor, V_2?

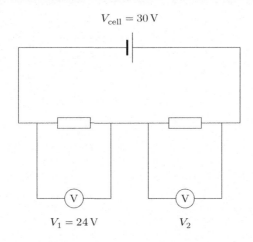

[2 marks]

151.) The diagram below shows a circuit. The potential difference provided by the cell, V_{cell}, is 33 V, the potential difference across the first resistor, V_1, is 21 V, and the potential difference across the second resistor, V_2, is 6 V. What is the potential difference across the third resistor, V_3?

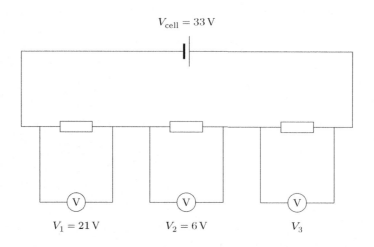

[2 marks]

152.) The diagram below shows a circuit. The potential difference provided by the cell, V_{cell}, is 2.1 V, and the potential difference across the second resistor, V_2, is 0.9 V.

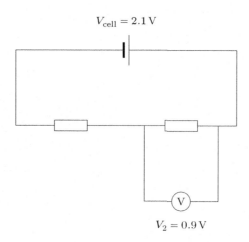

a.) Add, to the circuit, a voltmeter that would measure the potential difference across the first resistor, and give it the label V_1.

[1 mark]

b.) What is the potential difference across the first resistor, V_1?

_____

[**2 marks**]

153.) The diagram below shows a circuit. What is the potential difference across the second resistor, V_2?

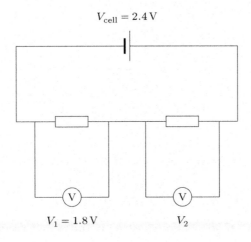

$V_{cell} = 2.4\,V$

$V_1 = 1.8\,V$ V_2

_____

[**3 marks**]

154.) The diagram below shows a circuit. What is the potential difference provided by the cell?

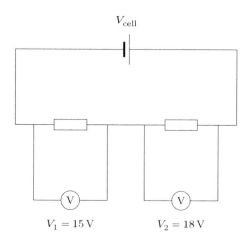

$V_1 = 15\,\text{V}$ $V_2 = 18\,\text{V}$

[3 marks]

155.) The diagram below shows a circuit. What is the potential difference provided by the cell?

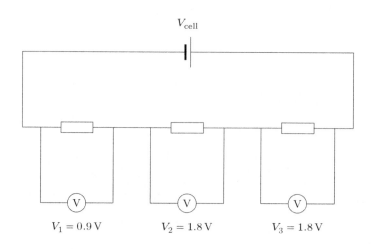

$V_1 = 0.9\,\text{V}$ $V_2 = 1.8\,\text{V}$ $V_3 = 1.8\,\text{V}$

[2 marks]

156.) The diagram below shows a circuit. What is the potential difference across the resistor?

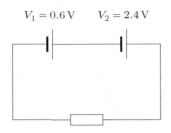

$V_1 = 0.6\,\text{V}$ $V_2 = 2.4\,\text{V}$

_____

[3 marks]

157.) The diagram below shows a circuit. What is the value of V_4?

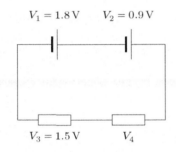

$V_1 = 1.8\,\text{V}$ $V_2 = 0.9\,\text{V}$

$V_3 = 1.5\,\text{V}$ V_4

_____

[4 marks]

158.) The diagram below shows a circuit. The two resistors in the circuit are identical. What is the potential difference across each resistor?

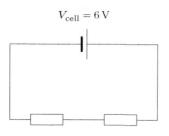

$V_{\text{cell}} = 6\,\text{V}$

[3 marks]

159.) The diagram below shows a circuit. The two resistors in the circuit are identical. What is the potential difference across each resistor?

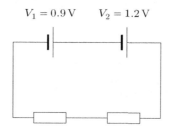

$V_1 = 0.9\,\text{V}$ $V_2 = 1.2\,\text{V}$

[4 marks]

160.) 4 860 Ω resistors are connected in series with a 23.2 V cell. Determine the potential difference across each resistor.

[3 marks]

161.) The diagram below shows a circuit consisting of two resistors connected in series with a cell.

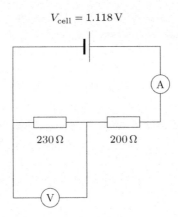

a.) What is the total resistance of the two resistors?

_____

[2 marks]

b.) What is the reading on the ammeter?

_____

[2 marks]

c.) What is the reading on the voltmeter?

_____

[2 marks]

162.) Below are shown two circuit diagrams. Are the circuit diagrams **equivalent**?

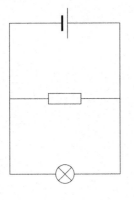
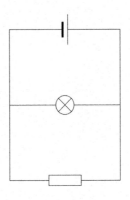

i.) Yes   ii.) No

[1 mark]

163.) Below are shown two circuit diagrams. Are the circuit diagrams **equivalent**?

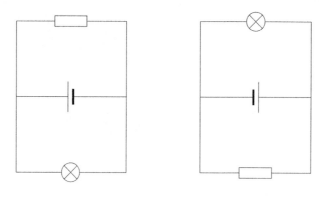

i.) Yes   ii.) No

[1 mark]

164.) Below are shown two circuit diagrams. Are the circuit diagrams **equivalent**?

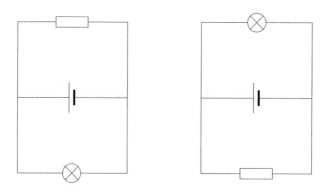

i.) Yes   ii.) No

[1 mark]

165.) Below are shown two circuit diagrams. Are the circuit diagrams **equivalent**?

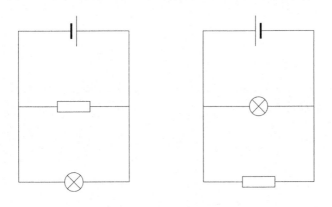

i.) Yes   ii.) No

[1 mark]

166.) The diagram below shows a circuit. The reading on the first ammeter, I_1, is 4.9 A, and the reading on the second ammeter, I_2, is 1 A. What is the reading on the third ammeter, I_3?

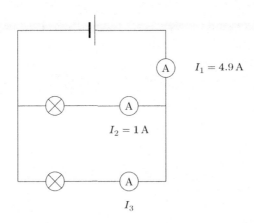

_____

[2 marks]

167.) The diagram below shows a circuit. The reading on the second ammeter, I_2, is 0.19 A, and the reading on the third ammeter, I_3, is 0.3 A. What is the reading on the first ammeter, I_1?

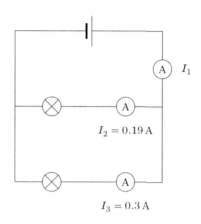

[2 marks]

168.) The diagram below shows a circuit. The reading on the first ammeter, I_1, is 0.58 A, the reading on the second ammeter, I_2, is 0.08 A, and the reading on the third ammeter, I_3, is 0.23 A. What is the reading on the fourth ammeter, I_4?

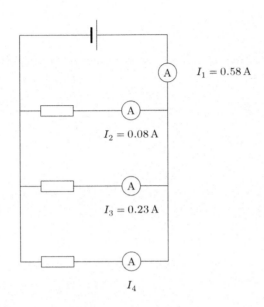

[2 marks]

169.) The diagram below shows a circuit. The reading on the second ammeter, I_2, is 1.3 A, the reading on the third ammeter, I_3, is 1.5 A, and the reading on the fourth ammeter, I_4, is 0.4 A. What is the reading on the first ammeter, I_1?

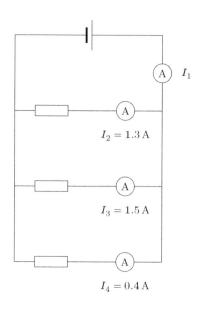

[2 marks]

170.) The diagram below shows a circuit. The potential difference provided by the cell is 7.1 V.

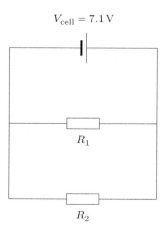

a.) What is the potential difference across the first resistor, R_1?

[2 marks]

b.) What is the potential difference across the second resistor, R_2?

_____

[2 marks]

171.) The diagram below shows a circuit. The potential difference across the first resistor, R_1, is 7.2 V.

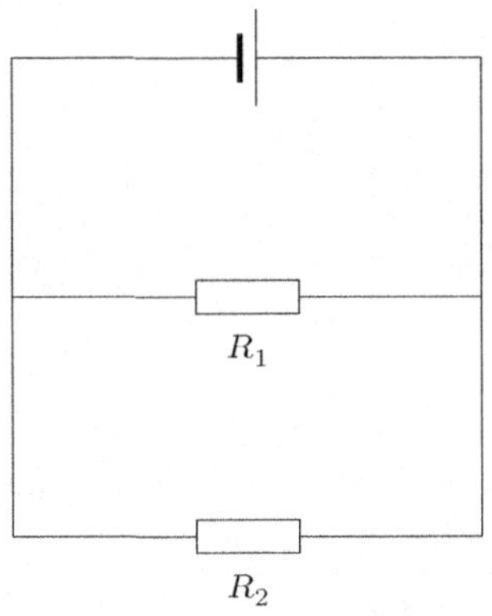

a.) What is the potential difference across the second resistor, R_2?

_____

[2 marks]

b.) What is the potential difference provided by the cell?

_____

[2 marks]

172.) The diagram below shows a circuit. If the switch is closed, does the potential difference across the first resistor, R_1, **increase**, **decrease**, or **stay the same**?

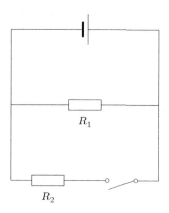

i.) It increases.

ii.) It decreases.

iii.) It stays the same.

[**2 marks**]

173.) The diagram below shows a circuit.

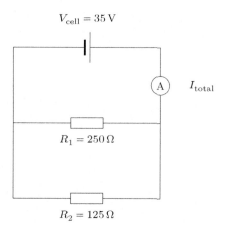

a.) What is the potential difference across resistor R_1?

_____

[**2 marks**]

b.) What is the current through resistor R_1?

_____

[2 marks]

c.) What is the potential difference across resistor R_2?

_____

[2 marks]

d.) What is the current through resistor R_2?

_____

[2 marks]

e.) What is the current through the ammeter, I_{total}?

_____

[2 marks]

174.) The diagram below shows a circuit.

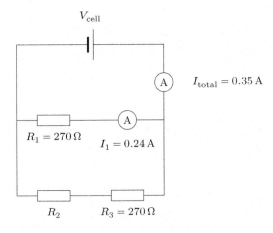

a.) What is the potential difference across resistor R_1?

_____

[2 marks]

b.) What is the current through resistor R_3?

[2 marks]

c.) What is the potential difference across resistor R_3?

[2 marks]

d.) What is the potential difference across resistor R_2?

[2 marks]

175.) The diagram below shows a circuit. What is the total resistance of the two resistors in the circuit? Give your answer to 3 significant figures.

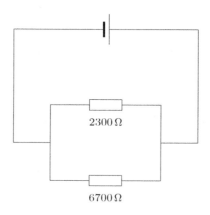

$2300\,\Omega$

$6700\,\Omega$

[3 marks]

176.) The diagram below shows a circuit. What is the total resistance of the two resistors in the circuit? Give your answer to 3 significant figures.

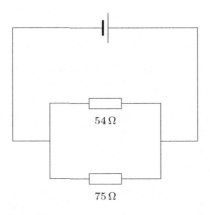

[3 marks]

177.) The diagram below shows a circuit. What is the total resistance of the two resistors in the circuit? Give your answer to 3 significant figures.

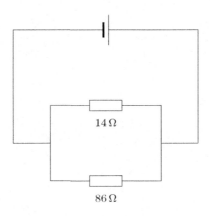

[3 marks]

178.) The diagram below shows a circuit. What is the total resistance of the two resistors in the circuit? Give your answer to 3 significant figures.

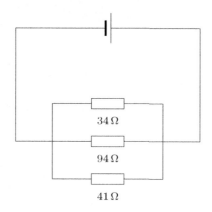

[3 marks]

179.) The diagram below shows a circuit. The total resistance of the two resistors is $9.77\,\Omega$. What is the value of R? Give your answer to 3 significant figures.

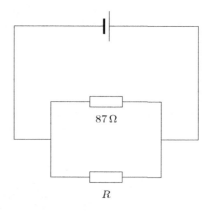

[3 marks]

180.) The diagram below shows a circuit. The total resistance of the three resistors is $1830\,\Omega$. What is the value of R? Give your answer to 3 significant figures.

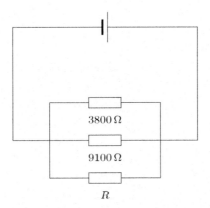

[3 marks]

181.) The diagram below shows a circuit. Two resistors are connected in parallel with the cell.

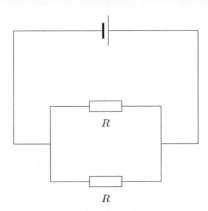

If a *third* resistor were connected in parallel with the other two, would the total resistance of the circuit **increase** or **decrease**?

i.) decrease   ii.) increase

[2 marks]

182.) The diagram below shows a circuit. Two resistors are connected in parallel with the cell.

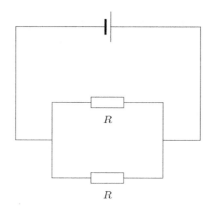

If a *third* resistor were connected in series with the existing pair, would the total resistance of the circuit **increase** or **decrease**?

   i.) decrease   ii.) increase

[2 marks]

183.) The diagram below shows a circuit. What is the total resistance of the three resistors in the circuit? Give your answer to 3 significant figures.

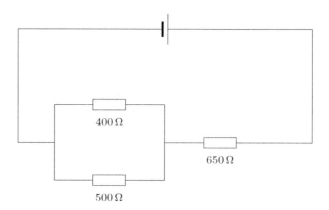

400 Ω

650 Ω

500 Ω

_____

[5 marks]

184.) The diagram below shows a circuit. What is the total resistance of the three resistors in the circuit? Give your answer to 3 significant figures.

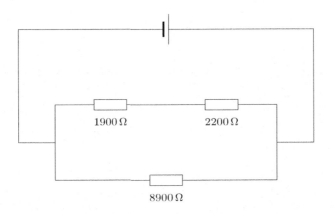

[5 marks]

185.) The diagram below shows a circuit.

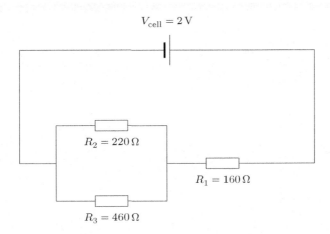

a.) What is the total resistance of the three resistors? Give your answer to 3 significant figures.

[5 marks]

b.) What is the current through R_1? Give your answer to 3 significant figures.

[3 marks]

c.) What is the potential difference across R_1? Give your answer to 3 significant figures.

_____

[3 marks]

d.) What is the potential difference across R_2? Give your answer to 3 significant figures.

_____

[3 marks]

e.) What is the current through R_2? Give your answer to 3 significant figures.

_____

[3 marks]

f.) What is the current through R_3? Give your answer to 3 significant figures.

_____

[3 marks]

186.) What is the S.I. unit of **energy**?

_____

[1 mark]

187.) Write the symbol for **joules**?

_____

[1 mark]

188.) Write the symbol for **kilojoules**?

_____

[1 mark]

189.) Write the symbol for **megajoules**?

_____

[1 mark]

190.) Write the symbol for **gigajoules**?

_____

[1 mark]

191.) What is $87.1\,\text{GJ}$ in joules?

  i.) $8.71 \times 10^{12}\,\text{J}$ ii.) $8.71 \times 10^{10}\,\text{J}$ iii.) $8.71 \times 10^{8}\,\text{J}$ iv.) $8.71 \times 10^{9}\,\text{J}$

[1 mark]

192.) What is $29.1\,\text{kJ}$ in joules?

  i.) $291000\,\text{J}$ ii.) $2910000\,\text{J}$ iii.) $2910\,\text{J}$ iv.) $29100\,\text{J}$

[1 mark]

193.) What is $4 \times 10^{7}\,\text{J}$ in gigajoules?

  i.) $0.0004\,\text{GJ}$ ii.) $0.4\,\text{GJ}$ iii.) $0.004\,\text{GJ}$ iv.) $0.04\,\text{GJ}$

[1 mark]

194.) What is $6800000\,\text{J}$ in megajoules?

  i.) $68\,\text{MJ}$ ii.) $680\,\text{MJ}$ iii.) $6.8\,\text{MJ}$ iv.) $0.068\,\text{MJ}$

[1 mark]

195.) What is $21.8\,\text{GJ}$ in kilojoules?

  i.) $2180000\,\text{kJ}$ ii.) $2.18 \times 10^{7}\,\text{kJ}$ iii.) $2.18 \times 10^{8}\,\text{kJ}$ iv.) $218000\,\text{kJ}$

[1 mark]

196.) What is $81.7\,\text{MJ}$ in kilojoules?

  i.) $8170000\,\text{kJ}$ ii.) $81700\,\text{kJ}$ iii.) $8170\,\text{kJ}$ iv.) $817\,\text{kJ}$

[1 mark]

197.) What is $8000000\,\text{kJ}$ in gigajoules?

  i.) $8\,\text{GJ}$ ii.) $800\,\text{GJ}$ iii.) $0.8\,\text{GJ}$ iv.) $0.08\,\text{GJ}$

[1 mark]

198.) Complete the following sentence.

One joule is equal to the energy required to move one _____ of charge across a potential difference of one _____.

[2 marks]

199.) Which of the following is equivalent to 1 J?

i.) $1\,CV$

iii.) $1\,Cs$

ii.) $1\,\frac{C}{V}$

iv.) $1\,\frac{V}{C}$

[1 mark]

200.) Which of the following are measures of **energy**?

i.) 700 W	iv.) 66.5 W	vii.) 20.8 J	x.) 115 mA
ii.) 22.6 V	v.) 98.3 kJ	viii.) 3.61 A	xi.) 88 mV
iii.) 755 J	vi.) 3.98 MJ	ix.) 25.3 mA	xii.) 70.4 kW

[1 mark]

201.) The formula $E = QV$ gives the energy, E, required to move an amount of charge Q across a potential difference V. Rearrange this formula to make Q the subject.

[2 marks]

202.) How much energy is required to move 9.6 C across a potential difference of 22.3 V?

[2 marks]

203.) How much energy is required to move 6.2 C across a potential difference of 12.5 V?

[2 marks]

204.) How much energy is required to move $8.8\,\text{mC}$ across a potential difference of $15.5\,\text{V}$?

_____

[2 marks]

205.) $11.7\,\text{mC}$ of charge is moved across a potential difference of V. It takes $0.11349\,\text{J}$ of energy to do so. What is the value of V?

_____

[3 marks]

206.) An amount of charge, q, is moved across a potential difference of $4.5\,\text{V}$. It takes $0.0342\,\text{J}$ of energy to do so. What is the value of q?

_____

[3 marks]

207.) An amount of charge, q, is moved across a potential difference of $8\,\text{V}$. It takes $18.4\,\text{J}$ of energy to do so. What is the value of q?

_____

[3 marks]

208.) The diagram below shows a circuit.

$$V = 7\,\text{V}$$

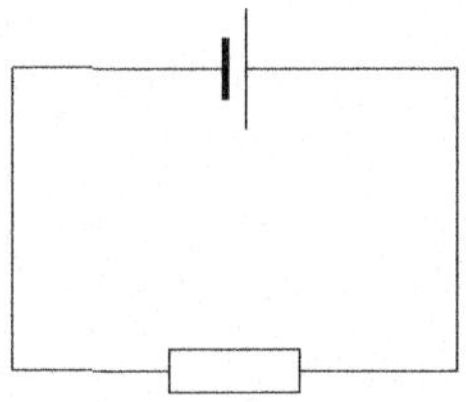

How much charge must pass through the resistor for $1.407\,\text{J}$ of energy to be dissipated into the environment? Give your answer in millicoulombs.

_____

[3 marks]

209.) The diagram below shows a circuit.

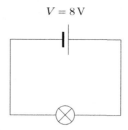

$$V = 8\,\text{V}$$

If $421\,\text{mC}$ of charge passes through the bulb, how much energy is released by the bulb as light and heat?

_____

[**3 marks**]

210.) $9.6\,\text{C}$ of charge is moved across a potential difference of V. It takes $192.96\,\text{J}$ of energy to do so. What is the value of V?

_____

[**3 marks**]

211.) The diagram below shows a circuit.

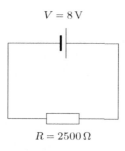

$$V = 8\,\text{V}$$

$$R = 2500\,\Omega$$

a.) What is the current through the resistor?

_____

[**3 marks**]

b.) How much charge passes through the resistor in $27\,\text{s}$?

_____

[2 marks]

c.) How much energy is dissipated by the resistor in 27 s?

_____

[2 marks]

212.) The diagram below shows a circuit.

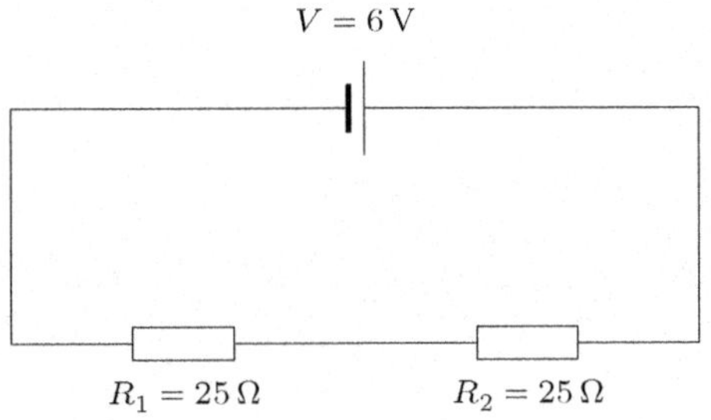

$V = 6\,\text{V}$

$R_1 = 25\,\Omega$ $R_2 = 25\,\Omega$

a.) What is the total resistance of the two resistors?

_____

[3 marks]

b.) What is the current in the circuit?

_____

[2 marks]

c.) What is the potential difference across R_2?

_____

[2 marks]

d.) How much charge passes through R_2 in 22 s?

_____

[2 marks]

e.) How much energy is dissipated by R_2 in 22 s?

_____

[2 marks]

213.) Define **power**.

_____

_____

[2 marks]

214.) What is the S.I. unit of **power**?

  i.) the ohm   ii.) the joule   iii.) the watt   iv.) the coulomb

[1 mark]

215.) Which of the following is the correct symbol for **watts**?

  i.) V   ii.) J   iii.) w   iv.) W

[1 mark]

216.) What is 15.7 GW in watts?

  i.) 1.57×10^8 W   ii.) 1.57×10^{10} W   iii.) 1.57×10^{12} W   iv.) 1.57×10^{11} W

[1 mark]

217.) What is 7.9 kW in watts?

  i.) 79 W   ii.) 790000 W   iii.) 7900 W   iv.) 79000 W

[1 mark]

218.) What is 76000 W in megawatts?

  i.) 7.6 MW   ii.) 0.076 MW   iii.) 0.0076 MW   iv.) 0.76 MW

[1 mark]

219.) What is 72.8 MW in watts?

  i.) 7.28×10^8 W   ii.) 7.28×10^9 W   iii.) 7.28×10^7 W   iv.) 728000 W

[1 mark]

220.) What is 10000 kW in gigawatts?

  i.) 1 GW   ii.) 0.0001 GW   iii.) 0.001 GW   iv.) 0.01 GW

[1 mark]

221.) What is $50.7\,\text{GW}$ in megawatts?

   i.) $507\,\text{MW}$ ii.) $507000\,\text{MW}$ iii.) $5070000\,\text{MW}$ iv.) $50700\,\text{MW}$

[1 mark]

222.) What is $290000\,\text{MW}$ in gigawatts?

   i.) $290\,\text{GW}$ ii.) $29\,\text{GW}$ iii.) $2900\,\text{GW}$ iv.) $29000\,\text{GW}$

[1 mark]

223.) Complete the following sentence.

One watt is equal to one _____ of energy transferred in one _____.

[2 marks]

224.) Which of the following is equivalent to 1 watt?

   i.) $1\,\frac{\text{s}}{\text{J}}$ iii.) $1\,\frac{\text{C}}{\text{s}}$

   ii.) $1\,\frac{\text{J}}{\text{s}}$ iv.) $1\,\text{Js}$

[1 mark]

225.) Which of the following are measures of **power**?

   i.) $11.7\,\text{V}$ iv.) $840\,\text{mV}$ vii.) $34.9\,\text{W}$ x.) $11\,\text{V}$

   ii.) $8.19\,\text{MW}$ v.) $34.6\,\text{kW}$ viii.) $59.3\,\text{J}$ xi.) $64\,\text{mV}$

   iii.) $665\,\text{J}$ vi.) $35\,\text{mA}$ ix.) $830\,\text{W}$ xii.) $3.52\,\text{MJ}$

[1 mark]

226.) The formula $P = \frac{E}{t}$ relates the power of an electrical component, P, to the energy transferred by it, E, in time t. Rearrange this formula to make E the subject.

_____

[2 marks]

227.) A filament lamp in a circuit transfers $2200\,\text{J}$ of energy in $10\,\text{s}$. What is the power of the filament lamp?

_____

[2 marks]

228.) A filament lamp in a circuit transfers 2700 J of energy in 30 s. Calculate the power of the filament lamp.

_____

[2 marks]

229.) A filament lamp in a circuit transfers 441000 J of energy in 1.75 h. What is the power of the filament lamp?

_____

[3 marks]

230.) A filament lamp in a circuit transfers 63000 J of energy in 10.5 min. What is the power of the filament lamp?

_____

[3 marks]

231.) A filament lamp in a circuit has a power of 150 W. How much energy is transferred by the filament lamp in 28 s?

_____

[2 marks]

232.) A filament lamp in a circuit has a power of 270 W. Determine the energy transferred by the filament lamp in 3 min.

_____

[3 marks]

233.) A filament lamp in a circuit has a power of 280 mW. How much energy is transferred by the filament lamp in 2 h?

_____

[3 marks]

234.) The formula $P = IV$ relates the power of an electrical component, P, to the potential difference across it, V, and the current through it, I. Rearrange this formula to make I the subject.

_____

[2 marks]

235.) A resistor in a circuit has a potential difference across it of 5.5 V and a current through it of 3.2 A. What is the power of the resistor?

_____

[2 marks]

236.) The diagram below shows a circuit.

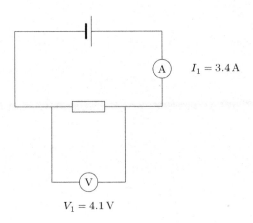

$I_1 = 3.4\,\text{A}$

$V_1 = 4.1\,\text{V}$

What is the power of the resistor?

_____

[2 marks]

237.) The diagram below shows a circuit.

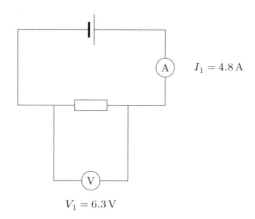

$I_1 = 4.8\,\text{A}$

$V_1 = 6.3\,\text{V}$

What is the power of the resistor?

_____

[2 marks]

238.) The diagram below shows a circuit.

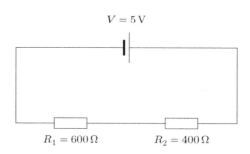

$V = 5\,\text{V}$

$R_1 = 600\,\Omega$ $R_2 = 400\,\Omega$

a.) What is the total resistance of the two resistors?

_____

[3 marks]

b.) What is the current in the circuit?

_____

[2 marks]

c.) What is the potential difference across R_1?

_____

[2 marks]

d.) What is the power of R_1?

_____

[2 marks]

e.) What is the potential difference across R_2?

_____

[2 marks]

f.) What is the power of R_2?

_____

[2 marks]

239.) The diagram below shows a circuit.

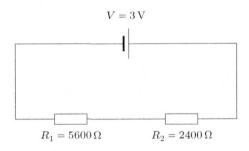

$V = 3\,\mathrm{V}$

$R_1 = 5600\,\Omega$ $R_2 = 2400\,\Omega$

What is the power of R_1?

_____

[9 marks]

240.) The diagram below shows a circuit.

$V_{\text{cell}} = 9.5\,\text{V}$

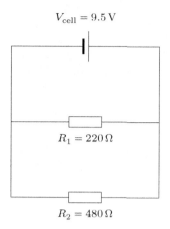

$R_1 = 220\,\Omega$

$R_2 = 480\,\Omega$

a.) What is the current through R_1. Give your answer to 3 significant figures.

_____

[4 marks]

b.) What is the power of R_1? Give your answer to 3 significant figures.

_____

[3 marks]

241.) The diagram below shows a circuit.

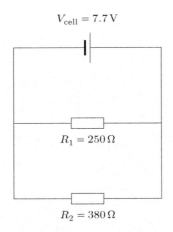

$V_{\text{cell}} = 7.7\,\text{V}$

$R_1 = 250\,\Omega$

$R_2 = 380\,\Omega$

What is the power of R_1? Give your answer to 3 significant figures.

_____

[4 marks]

242.) Which of the following formulae correctly relates the power of an electrical component, P, to its resistance, R, and the current through it, I?

i.) $P = IR$
ii.) $P = \frac{I}{R}$

iii.) $P = \frac{I^2}{R}$
iv.) $P = I^2R$

[1 mark]

243.) A resistor with a resistance of $340\,\Omega$ has a current through it of $3.8\,\text{A}$. Determine the power of the resistor.

_____

[2 marks]

244.) A resistor with a resistance of $180\,\Omega$ has a current through it of $3.7\,\text{A}$. Determine the power of the resistor.

_____

[2 marks]

245.) The diagram below shows a circuit.

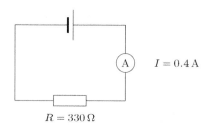

$R = 330\,\Omega$

What is the power of the resistor? Give your answer to 3 significant figures.

_____

[3 marks]

246.) Which of the following formulae correctly relates the power of an electrical component, P, to its resistance, R, and the potential difference across it, V?

i.) $P = \frac{V}{R}$ iii.) $P = VR^2$

ii.) $P = \frac{V^2}{R}$ iv.) $P = \frac{V}{R^2}$

[1 mark]

247.) A resistor with a resistance of $50\,\Omega$ has a potential difference across it of $27.9\,\mathrm{V}$. What is the power of the resistor? Give your answer to 3 significant figures.

_____

[2 marks]

248.) A resistor with a resistance of $435\,\Omega$ has a potential difference across it of $29.4\,\mathrm{V}$. What is the power of the resistor? Give your answer to 3 significant figures.

_____

[2 marks]

249.) The diagram below shows a circuit.

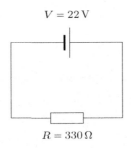

$$V = 22\,\text{V}$$

$$R = 330\,\Omega$$

What is the power of the resistor? Give your answer to 3 significant figures.

_____

[**3 marks**]

250.) The diagram below shows a circuit.

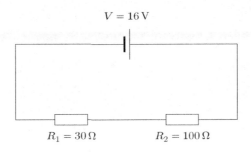

$$V = 16\,\text{V}$$

$$R_1 = 30\,\Omega \qquad R_2 = 100\,\Omega$$

What is the total power of the two resistors? Give your answer to 3 significant figures.

_____

[**4 marks**]

ANSWERS

1.) a resistor

2.) a fuse

3.) a filament lamp / bulb

4.) a cell

5.) a battery

6.) an open switch

7.)

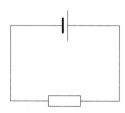

8.)

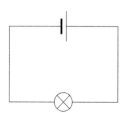

9.)

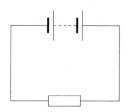

10.) No

11.) Yes

12.) No

13.) Yes

14.) Yes

15.) No

16.) No

17.) No

18.) Yes

19.) No

20.) Yes

21.) Yes

22.) a photovoltaic cell

23.) a diode

24.) a light-emitting diode

25.) a variable resistor

26.) a thermistor

27.) a light-dependent resistor

28.)

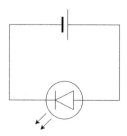

29.)

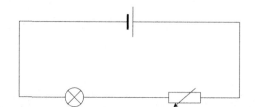

30.) a capacitor

31.) in series

32.) in parallel

33.) in series

34.) in series

35.)

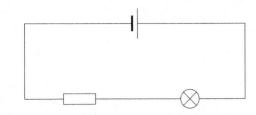

36.)

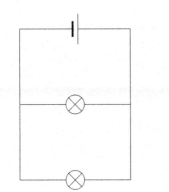

37.)

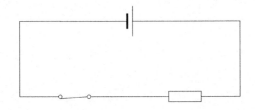

38.) electric charge

39.) In a circuit that has an electric current, the negatively-charged electrons in the wire **do** move, but the positively-charged atomic nuclei **don't** move.

40.) the coulomb

41.) the ampere

42.) One **coulomb** of charge moving past a point in a circuit in one **second** is one **ampere** of current.

43.) C

44.) A

45.) s

46.) 1000

47.) 1000

48.) mC

49.) mA

50.) 22.4 C , 285 C , 248 mC , 1150 mC

51.) 1.1 A , 0.71 A , 261 mA , 226 mA

52.) 6.785 C

53.) 9.305 C

54.) 119300 mC

55.) 23600 mC

56.) 8.68 A

57.) 5.085 A

58.) 7960 mA

59.) 3010 mA

60.) Direct current is current with a constant direction and magnitude.

61.) Alternating current is current that periodically reverses direction.

62.) direct current

63.) alternating current

64.) alternating current

65.) direct current

66.) direct current

67.) alternating current

68.)

69.) a.) clockwise

69.) b.) anticlockwise

70.) a.) anticlockwise

70.) b.) clockwise

71.) a.) clockwise

71.) b.) anticlockwise

72.) The conventional current in a circuit is in the **opposite direction** to the motion of the electrons.

73.) an ammeter

74.) In order to measure the current through a component, an ammeter must be connected **in series** with the component.

75.)

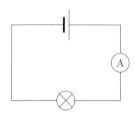

76.) 4.6 A

77.) 8 A

78.) 85 C

79.) 1.1 A

80.) 15 s

81.) 80 s

82.) 70 C

83.) 4.4 A

84.) 55.5 min

85.) 4662 C

86.) 200 mA

87.) A diode is a type of circuit component that only allows current through it in one direction.

88.) A light-emitting diode is a diode that emits light when charge flows through it.

89.) Yes

90.) No

91.) Yes

92.) No

93.) Electrical resistance is the opposition to the flow of electric charge. The greater the electrical resistance of a component, the harder it is for charge to flow through it.

94.) the ohm

95.) omega

96.) Ω

97.) 1000

98.) 1000

99.) 1000000

100.) kΩ

101.) MΩ

102.) $475\,\Omega$, $920\,\Omega$, $25.1\,\text{k}\Omega$, $9.9\,\text{M}\Omega$

103.) $32600\,\Omega$

104.) $18900\,\Omega$

105.) $20\,\text{k}\Omega$

106.) $78\,\text{k}\Omega$

107.) $77\,\text{M}\Omega$

108.) $43\,\text{M}\Omega$

109.) $6.37 \times 10^7\,\Omega$

110.) $6.25 \times 10^7\,\Omega$

111.) $29\,\text{M}\Omega$

112.) $7\,\text{M}\Omega$

113.) an ohmmeter

114.) an ohmmeter

115.) the volt

116.) V

117.) 22100 V

118.) 7400 V

119.) 6 kV

120.) 10.2 kV

121.) a voltmeter

122.) In order to measure the potential difference across a component, a voltmeter must be connected **in parallel** with the component.

123.)

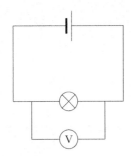

124.) a.) $I = \frac{V}{R}$

124.) b.) Ohm's Law

125.) 0.26 A

126.) $R = \frac{V}{I}$

127.) 55 Ω

128.) $V = IR$

129.) 4.2 V

130.) 24.7 V

131.) 0.36 A

132.) 95 Ω

133.) 170 Ω

134.) a.)

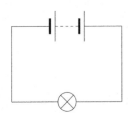

134.) b.) 0.29 A

134.) c.) 84.1 C

135.) 50

136.) 100 Ω

137.) $R_{\text{total}} = R_1 + R_2 + R_3 + \ldots$

138.) 61 Ω

139.) 590 Ω

140.) 58 Ω

141.) 620 Ω

142.) 46 Ω

143.) 460 Ω

144.) 35 Ω

145.) 320 Ω

146.) 0.01 A

147.) 0.88 A

148.) $I_1 = I_2$

149.) $I_1 = I_2 = I_3$

150.) 6 V

151.) 6 V

152.) a.)

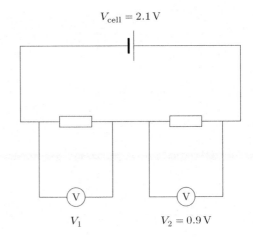

$V_{\text{cell}} = 2.1\,\text{V}$

V_1 $V_2 = 0.9\,\text{V}$

152.) b.) 1.2 V

153.) 0.6 V

154.) 33 V

155.) 4.5 V

156.) 3 V

157.) 1.2 V

158.) 3 V

159.) 1.05 V

160.) 5.8 V

161.) a.) 430 Ω

161.) b.) 0.0026 A

161.) c.) 0.598 V

162.) Yes

163.) Yes

164.) Yes

165.) Yes

166.) 3.9 A

167.) 0.49 A

168.) 0.27 A

169.) 3.2 A

170.) a.) 7.1 V

170.) b.) 7.1 V

171.) a.) 7.2 V

171.) b.) 7.2 V

172.) It stays the same.

173.) a.) 35 V

173.) b.) 0.14 A

173.) c.) 35 V

173.) d.) 0.28 A

173.) e.) 0.42 A

174.) a.) 64.8 V

174.) b.) 0.11 A

174.) c.) 29.7 V

174.) d.) 35.1 V

175.) 1710 Ω

176.) 31.4 Ω

177.) 12 Ω

178.) 15.5 Ω

179.) 11 Ω

180.) 5770 Ω

181.) decrease

182.) increase

183.) 872 Ω

184.) 2810 Ω

185.) a.) 309 Ω

185.) b.) 0.00648 A

185.) c.) 1.04 V

185.) d.) 0.96 V

185.) e.) 0.00436 A

185.) f.) 0.00212 A

186.) the joule

187.) J

188.) kJ

189.) MJ

190.) GJ

191.) 8.71×10^{10} J

192.) 29100 J

193.) 0.04 GJ

194.) 6.8 MJ

195.) 2.18×10^{7} kJ

196.) 81700 kJ

197.) 8 GJ

198.) One joule is equal to the energy required to move one coulomb of charge across a potential difference of one volt.

199.) 1 CV

200.) 20.8 J , 755 J , 98.3 kJ , 3.98 MJ

201.) $Q = \frac{E}{V}$

202.) 214.08 J

203.) 77.5 J

204.) 0.1364 J

205.) 9.7 V

206.) 7.6 mC

207.) 2.3 C

208.) 201 mC

209.) 3.368 J

210.) 20.1 V

211.) a.) 0.0032 A

211.) b.) 0.0864 C

211.) c.) 0.6912 J

212.) a.) 50 Ω

212.) b.) 0.12 A

212.) c.) 3 V

212.) d.) 2.64 C

212.) e.) 7.92 J

213.) The power of an electrical component is the amount of energy transferred by it per unit time.

214.) the watt

215.) W

216.) 1.57×10^{10} W

217.) 7900 W

218.) 0.076 MW

219.) 7.28×10^7 W

220.) 0.01 GW

221.) 50700 MW

222.) 290 GW

223.) One watt is equal to one joule of energy transferred in one second.

224.) $1 \frac{J}{s}$

225.) 34.9 W , 830 W , 34.6 kW , 8.19 MW

226.) $E = Pt$

227.) 220 W

228.) 90 W

229.) 70 W

230.) 100 W

231.) 4200 J

232.) 48600 J

233.) 2016 J

234.) $I = \frac{P}{V}$

235.) 17.6 W

236.) 13.94 W

237.) 30.24 W

238.) a.) 1000 Ω

238.) b.) 0.005 A

238.) c.) 3 V

238.) d.) 0.015 W

238.) e.) 2 V

238.) f.) 0.01 W

239.) 0.0007875 W

240.) a.) 0.0432 A

240.) b.) 0.41 W

241.) 0.237 W

242.) $P = I^2 R$

243.) 4909.6 W

244.) 2464.2 W

245.) 52.8 W

246.) $P = \frac{V^2}{R}$

247.) 15.6 W

248.) 1.99 W

249.) 1.47 W

250.) 1.97 W

DID YOU LIKE THIS BOOK?

If you liked this book, consider giving it a review where you bought it. This will help others to find the book.

Printed in Great Britain
by Amazon

32269350R00057